DIABETIC COOKBOOK
50 DIABETIC FRIENDLY RECIPES

A DIABETES DIET THAT IS DELICIOUS

BREAKFAST, LUNCH, DINNER, & DESSERT

RECIPES

MARIA VEGA

These recipes were written by a daughter of a diabetic who helps her mother who suffers from diabetes. These recipes are not intended to be Medical advice, nor are the recipes written for any specific type of diabetic. Always consult your Medical Doctor before adding or taking away anything from your diet.

Table of Contents

Delicious Chicken Salad Lunch Wrap

The Ultimate Power Salad

Red Pepper and Arugula Panini

Savory Ginger and Sweet Potato Soup

Veggie and Cheese Pitas

Traditional Tuna Pasta Salad

Traditional Black Bean Mexican Soup

Mini Pepper and Asparagus Quiche

Vegetarian Chili

Broccoli Cream Soup

Classic Mediterranean Turkey Wrap

Lettuce and Shrimp Wraps

Hearty Mozzarella and Chickpea Salad

Spicy Watermelon Salad With Baked Catfish

Chicken in Tomato Basil Soup

Black Bean Vegetarian Burgers

Nutritious Spinach and Pasta Shells

Delicious Desserts

Yummy Quinoa Pudding

Watermelon and Strawberry Frozen Dessert

Pumpkin Panna Cotta

Berry and Chocolate Parfait

Smore Shooters

Delicious Mini Pumpkin Tarts

Traditional Apple Crisp

Delicious Trifle Pudding

Low Fat Style Crème Brule

Mouthwatering Frozen Greek Yogurt

Almond Flavored Hot Chocolate

Baked Cinnamon Apples

Pumpkin Bread Pudding

Strawberries Dipped In Balsamic Vinegar

Banana and Chocolate Tofu Pudding

Sugar Free Applesauce Cake

Hey one more thing!

Breakfast Recipes

Classic Eggs and Toast

This prefect and low budget recipe can be served alongside a small side salad with some balsamic vinaigrette to make one of the healthiest and diabetic breakfast meals you will ever have.

Calories: 240
Serving Size: 4

Ingredients:

- 4 Large Eggs, White
- 4 Slices of Bread, Whole Grain
- 1 Medium Sized Avocado, Mashed
- ¼ tsp. Black Pepper
- ¼ tsp. Salt, For Taste
- ¼ cup of Plain Yogurt, Greek and Low fat

Directions:

1. Poach Your Egg-to do this fill a microwavable bowl with 1 cup water and crack one egg into the water, submerging it completely. Cover and microwave for 1 minute or until both the white and the yolk are starting to set.

2. Toast your whole grain slices of bread. Top toast with ¼ of your mashed avocado. Sprinkle with a dash of salt and pepper for taste.

3. Next place your poached egg on top of the avocado and place a dollop of yogurt onto the egg. Serve and enjoy.

Delicious Fruit Parfait

Whether you are looking for a small and easy recipe to make or are looking for a recipe that will help you kick start your morning in a healthy way, you are certainly going to love this recipe.

Calories: 245
Serving Size: 4

Ingredients:

- 4 Cups of Blueberries and Strawberries, Fresh
- 24 Ounces of Light Vanilla Yogurt, Fat Free
- 1 Cup Honey Bunches of Oats Cereal

Directions:

1. In a small juice glass scoop about 3 ounces of your fat free Vanilla yogurt, ¼ of your berry mix and a sprinkle of the cereal. Mix to combine and continue process for the remainder of the parfait glasses you are making.

2. Serve with a large glass of orange juice and enjoy.

Savory Ham and Egg Breakfast Burrito

If you are the kind of person who is tired of making the same breakfast dish every day, you are going to certainly like this recipe. Not only is this burrito very fulfilling, but it will leave you craving more.

Calories: 200

Serving Size: 4

Ingredients:

- 4 Eggs, Large
- 4 Egg Whites
- Dash of Hot Sauce For Taste
- 2 tsp. of Fat Free and Trans Fat Free Butter
- 2 Tbsp. of Shredded Cheddar Cheese, Reduced Fat
- ¼ cup of Onion, Diced Into Small Pieces
- ¼ cup of Green Peppers, Diced Into Small Pieces
- 4 tsp. of Salas, your favorite brand

- 4 Large Corn Tortillas, Heated
- 4 Slices of Ham, Reduced Sodium
- Dash of Pepper For Taste

Directions:

1. In a mixing bowl add in your eggs, egg whites, shredded cheese, hot sauce and black pepper. Whisk together or until thoroughly blended.

2. In a saucepan heat up your fat free butter over medium to high heat. Add your ham into the saucepan and sauté for only 3 minutes. Remove your ham from heat. Next add in your diced peppers and onion and cook over heat for the next 5 minutes. Reduce heat and add your ham back into the pan.

3. Next add your eggs into your saucepan and stir continuously until your eggs are fully scrambled and cooked.

4. Divide up your eggs and ham mixture and spoon a good amount into the center of your corn tortilla. Top your egg mixture with salsa and fold your tortilla into a burrito. Serve and enjoy.

Yummy Wheat Breakfast Pizza

Who says that you can only eat pizza for lunch or dinner? With this delicious recipe you can enjoy your favorite kind of food with the most nutritious toppings ever.

Calories: 170
Serving Size: 2

Ingredients:

- 2 Button Mushrooms, sliced into fine slices
- ½ cup of Your Favorite Egg Substitute
- 1 tsp. of Light and Fat Free Butter
- 2 Green Onion, Chopped Finely
- 2 Tbsp. of Milk, Fat-Free
- ½ Red Bell Pepper, Diced Into Small Pieces
- 1 Tomato, Small, De-seeded and Chopped Into Tiny Pieces
- 1 Whole Grain English Muffin, Cut In Half

- ¼ cup of Colby and Monterey Jack Cheese, Low-Fat

Directions:

1. Preheat your over to 375 degrees. Next take a small skillet that is non-stick and heat your butter over medium to low heat until it melts. Coat the entire bottom of the pan with the butter. Sauté your mushrooms, pepper and onion for about 3 minutes or until the mixture is tender.

2. In a separate bowl whisk your fat free milk and egg substitute together until thoroughly whisked. Add to your skillet with vegetables and let it cook without stirring. While the egg sets tilt the skillet to ensure that any runny egg mixture is cooked thoroughly. It should take about 3 to 4 minutes for egg mixture to fully set.

3. On a cookie sheet place your English muffin halves face up and sprinkle with some Monterey Jack and Colby cheese. Spoon your egg mixture onto the English Muffins and top with more cheese and tomato.

4. Place English muffins into you oven and allow to bake until the cheese fully melts. Serve with a bowl of fruit and enjoy.

Delicious Breakfast Nachos

Who says that you can only enjoy nachos for a snack? With this recipe you will be able to enjoy nachos as soon as the sun rises and it is a recipe that your entire family will enjoy. Not only is it delicious, but it is healthy as well.

Calories: 225
Serving Size: 4

Ingredients:

- 6 Eggs, Whites Only
- 1 1/3 cup of Refried Beans, Fat-Free
- 2 tsp. of Your Favorite Hot Sauce
- ¼ tsp. Black Pepper For Taste
- ¼ cup of Milk, Skim
- ½ Cup of Fresh Salsa
- 1 Avocado, Mashed Until Smooth
- ½ cup of Shredded Mozzarella Cheese, Reduced Fat

- 4 Ounces of Tortilla Chips, Baked
- 1 Tbsp. of Margarine, Trans Fat Free and Fat Free

Directions:

1. In a small saucepan, heat up your refried beans until they are piping hot.

2. Using a medium sized mixing bowl whisk together your egg whites, black pepper and hot sauce until the mixture becomes frothy.

3. In a non-stick skillet melt your margarine and make sure the entire bottom of the skillet is covered. Next pour in your egg mixture and constantly stir to ensure your eggs are scrambled. Continue until fully coked.

4. Next divide up your chips among as many plates as you need and pour hot beans onto the chips. Sprinkle some Mozzarella cheese on top and pour egg mixture onto the cheese. Top each plate you have made with fresh salsa and some mashed avocado and serve. Enjoy.

Baked Eggs With Feta, Spinach and Tomato

There is nothing better than to wake up to a nice and hearty healthy egg breakfast. We are certain you are going to love this recipe.

Calories: 75
Serving Size: 4

Ingredients:

- Some cooking spray
- 4 Eggs, Medium Sized
- ¼ cup of Tomato, Diced Into Small Pieces
- 1 tsp. of Fresh Oregano, Minced
- ½ cup of Spinach, Finely Chopped
- 2 Tbsp. of Feta Cheese, Fat-Free

Directions:

1. Preheat your oven to 375 degrees.

2. In your ramekins or small baking dishes, spray with enough cooking spray to coat them thoroughly.

3. Place your feta cheese, spinach, oregano and tomato into each dish and make sure they are all distributed evenly.

4. Place your egg on top of your spinach and oregano mixture. Place dishes into your oven and bake for 10 to 12 minutes or until the egg yolks are nice and soft.

5. Remove from oven and cool until warm and serve.

Fluffy Corn and Blueberry Muffins, Gluten Free Style

With a gluten free style, these muffins are sure to please even the pickiest of eaters. These muffins make a great on the go breakfast or an easy dish to make when you are feeling lazy.

Calories: 140
Serving Size: 22

Ingredients:

- Some cooking spray
- ¼ cup of Oil, Canola kind
- 1 Package of Cornbread mix
- 2 Egg Whites
- 1 Egg
- 1 ¾ cup of Buttermilk, Low-Fat
- 1 ½ cup of Fresh Blueberries
- ½ of Fresh Lemon, Juiced
- ½ tsp. of Vanilla

- ¼ cup of Splenda

Directions:

1. Preheat your oven to 375 degrees. While your oven heat up line your muffin tins with muffin papers and spray with a good amount of cooking spray.

2. In a separate mixing bowl combine your cornbread mix, egg whites, ¼ cup of Splenda, buttermilk, egg, and lemon juice. Mix until well blended.

3. Next fold in your blueberries gently until thoroughly combined

4. Spoon about ¼ cup of batter into each muffin cup and sprinkle with additional Splenda sugar.

5. Bake your muffins for about 22 minutes or until they are lightly browned on the top. Remove from oven and allow to cool on a wire rack before serving. Enjoy.

Healthy Asparagus Frittata

You can make this dish for either breakfast, lunch or dinner. This dish is pretty easy to make and will leave you wanting more.

Calories: 95
Serving Size: 6

Ingredients:

- Some cooking spray
- 1 whole container of Egg Substitute
- 1 Whole Bunch of Asparagus, Thin and Trimmed
- 1 Tbsp. of Olive Oil
- ¼ cup of Freshly Grated Parmesan Cheese
- ¼ tsp. of Black Pepper For Taste
- ¼ cup of Mozzarella Cheese, Shredded and Reduced Fat
- 2 Tbsp. of Milk, Skim
- 1/8 tsp. of Red Pepper Flakes

- 1 tsp. of Margarine, Trans Fat Free

Directions:

1. Preheat your oven to 425 degrees.

2. Spray a large baking sheet with some cooking spray. Meanwhile in a small mixing bowl toss your asparagus with some olive oil and place onto your baking sheet. Bake in your oven for about 12 minutes and then chop into small pieces. Set these aside.

3. In a separate mixing bowl combine your egg substitute, pepper, red pepper flakes and milk until thoroughly combined. Next spray a skillet with some cooking spray and your butter. Melt the butter. Add in your chopped asparagus and mixed egg mixture. Cook until the egg starts to set.

4. Add in both your Parmesan cheese and Mozzarella cheese. Cook until the mixture is almost set with the top still runny. Preheat your broiler.

5. Place newly made Frittata into broiler and broil until the top is golden brown in color. This should take about 2 to 4 minutes. Serve while still hot and enjoy.

Classic Hash Browns

These hash browns may be a little bit different then the ones you are familiar with as they are made with cauliflower. This recipe is absolutely delicious and will leave you and your family wanting more.

Calories: 100
Serving Size: 4

Ingredients:

- 1 Onion, Medium Sized and Diced Into Small Pieces
- 2 tsp. Vinegar, White Wine
- 1 ½ Tbsp. of Extra Virgin Olive Oil
- 1 Serrano Pepper, Minced
- 1 ½ Pounds of Small Cauliflower, Florets
- ½ tsp of Sea Salt, evenly divided
- ¼ cup of Fresh Parsley, Chopped Into Fine Pieces
- 2 Garlic Cloves, Minced

- 2 Scallions, Minced

- 2 tsp. of Fresh Rosemary, Finely Chopped

Directions:

1. In a large non-stick skillet, heat up your oil. Add in your cauliflower florets, diced onion, vinegar, salt and Serrano Pepper. Stir and cook until the cauliflower begins to caramelize, which usually takes about 7 minutes.

2. Next add in your minced garlic, scallions, chopped rosemary and sauté for an additional 1 to 2 minutes.

3. Next stir in your fresh parsley until thoroughly blended and serve while still piping hot. Enjoy.

Savory Spinach, Egg and Ham Sandwich

If you are looking for a recipe that is easy to make and that only require about 15 minutes to make it happen, this is certainly the recipe for you.

Calories: 234
Serving Size: 4

Ingredients:
- Some cooking spray
- ¼ tsp. of Garlic Powder
- 4 Slices of Ham, Smoked
- 4 Cups of Baby Spinach
- 4 Eggs
- 4 Whole Wheat Sandwich, Thins
- 1 Tbsp. of Olive Oil
- ¼ tsp. of Black Pepper
- 4 tsp. of Fresh Parmesan Cheese, Grated

Directions:

1. Using a non-stick and oven safe skillet, spray with a generous amount of cooking spray. Place on your stove and heat up. Add your ham slices and cook them for about 1 minute on each side.

2. Add your olive oil to the pan and your spinach. Sprinkle the spinach with garlic powder and black pepper. Sauté your baby spinach until the leaves become wilted and remove from pan.

3. Crack 1 egg at a time into your skillet and allow to cook for about 1 minute before flipping it. Sprinkle each egg with 1 tsp. of grated Parmesan Cheese and allow to cook thoroughly.

4. On your whole wheat slices place your cook spinach, ham and egg and cover. Eat while still warm.

Wholesome Granola

Granola is one of the best snacks that you can have throughout the day while on a diabetic diet. This recipe contains a perfect balance of protein and carbs and will leave you feeling incredibly full, especially after a good workout.

Calories: 200
Serving Size: 22

Ingredients:

- ¼ cup of Oil, Canola
- 1 Cup of Pecan, Chopped and Unsalted
- 1 Cup of Cashews, Chopped and Unsalted
- 1 Cup of Oats, Old Fashioned
- 1 Cup of Pumpkin Seeds, Raw and Unsalted
- ¼ Cup of Brown Sugar and Splenda, Blended Mix
- ¼ Cup of Peanut Butter
- 1 Cup of Sunflower Seeds, Unsalted

Directions:

1. Preheat your oven to 300 degrees.

2. Using a baking sheet, line it with some aluminum foil. Coat the foil with some cooking spray and set to the side.

3. In a bowl combine your pumpkin seeds, oats, cashews, pecans and sunflower seeds. Next pour your peanut butter over the mixture and stir thoroughly until it is all evenly coated.

4. Spread your newly created granola onto a single layer upon your baking sheet. Place in your owner and bake for the next 40-45 minutes, stirring constantly to ensure even browning throughout the process.

5. Remove from your oven and allow the granola to cool completely. Once cooled you can break it up into sizes according to your preference and store in a container. Enjoy whenever you wish.

Delicious Vanilla and Blackberry Waffles

Since this recipe incorporates the use of frozen waffles, you can rest assured that this will only take you a few minutes to put together. Easy and incredibly delicious.

Calories: 205
Serving Size: 6

Ingredients:

- 6 Frozen Waffles, Size of Your Choice
- 3 Tbsp. of Sugar
- ½ tsp. of Vanilla
- 1 Pound of Blackberries, Unsweetened and Frozen
- ½ tsp. of Lemon Zest
- ½ Cup of Vanilla Yogurt

Directions:

1. Toast your waffles and place onto as many plates as you need.

2. In a small mixing bowl combine your blackberries, vanilla, sugar and lemon zest. Spoon mixture on top of toasted waffles and add some vanilla yogurt on top of that. Serve while warm and enjoy.

Nutritious Blueberry Pancakes

Pancakes are the common go-to breakfast item and now with this recipe you can make something that is both delicious and nutritious for your entire family.

Calories: 150
Serving Size: 8

Ingredients:

- ¾ Cup Flour, All Purpose
- ¼ tsp. Salt (Optional)
- 1 Tbsp. of Splenda
- ¾ Cup of Flour, Whole Wheat
- 3 ½ tsp. of Baking Powder
- 1 ½ Cup of Milk, 1% or Buttermilk
- 1 Egg, Large
- 1 tsp. of Oil, Canola
- ½ tsp. of Vanilla Extract
- 1 Tbsp. of Applesauce, Unsweetened
- 1 Cup of Fresh Blueberries, Rinsed and Crushed

Directions:

1. In a large mixing bowl, combine both types of flour, splenda, salt (if you are using any) and baking powder with a whisk until thoroughly combined.

2. Next pour in you egg, milk, and egg and blend together until mixture is smooth. Last fold in your blueberries.

3. Spray a frying pan with a generous amount of cooking spray and pour some of your batter into it. Brown both sides of the pancake and serve while still hot. Top with some syrup and enjoy.

Oatmeal Ala Apple Pie Slowcooker Style

There is nothing better than Apple Pie and now with this recipe you can enjoy it every morning.

Calories: 234

Serves: 12

Ingredients:

- 3 Apples, Cored and Cut Into Small Pieces
- 3 Cups of Water
- 1 Cup of Apple Juice
- 1 Cup of Oats, Steel Cut
- ½ tsp. of Cinnamon, Ground

Directions:

1. Stir together you ground cinnamon, water, apple juice, chopped apples and oats in a slowcooker.

2. Cover and cook on the lowest setting for the next 4 to 6 hours or until the oats become tender. Serve while piping hot and enjoy.

Low Fat French Toast

With this recipe you can get the chance to enjoy your favorite Sunday breakfast without worrying about the harmful after effects.

Calories: 140
Serves: 6

Ingredients:

- 1 tsp. of Vanilla Extract
- 6 Slices of White Bread, Reduced Calories
- ½ Cup of Egg Substitute
- ½ tsp. of Cinnamon, Ground
- 2/3 Cup of Milk, Skim

Directions:

1. In a small bowl whisk together your egg substitute, ground cinnamon, milk and vanilla. Dip in your white bread slices until both sides are soaked with the egg substitute mixture.

2. In a separate saucepan spray it with a generous amount of cooking spray and heat up over low to medium low heat. Place your egg soaked bread slices into your pan and cook on both sides until golden brown. Sprinkle with some powdered sugar and serve while warm. Top with syrup and enjoy.

Classic Porridge

If you are a fan of traditional British dishes, you are going to love this recipe.

Calories: 140

Sevres: 4

Ingredients:

- 1 Cup of Oats, Rolled
- 1 tsp. of Salt (Optional)
- 2 Bananas, Peeled and Sliced
- 2 ½ Cups of Water
- 1 Tbsp. of Sugar
- ½ Cup of Milk
- A Dash Of Cinnamon For Taste

Directions:

1. In a medium sized saucepan mix together your sugar, oats, water, bananas, salt and cinnamon. Bring this to a rolling boil then reduce to a simmer until most of the liquid has been absorbed. Stir as frequently as possible and serve into bowl when done. Enjoy.

Colorful Fruit Salad

The best and healthy kind of breakfast that you could ever eat is the fruit salad. With this recipe you will be able to make an attractive looking fruit salad that will get even the pickiest of eaters to give it a try.

Calories: 135

Serves: 10

Ingredients:

- 1 Whole Cantaloupe, Seeded and Peeled
- ½ of a Watermelon
- 4 Plums, Pitted and Chopped Into Balls
- 1 Cup of Green Grapes, Seedless
- 1 Cup of Red Grapes, Seedless
- 1, 15 Ounce Can of Pineapple, Chunks and Drained
- 1 Pint of Fresh Blueberries, Drained and Rinsed

Directions:

1. Using a mellon baller, you will want to take your cantaloupe and your watermelon and hollow them out so they both create a large bowl.

2. Add your remaining ingredients to the melon bowls and gently mix together. Serve while still cold.

Lunch and Dinner Recipes

Delicious Chicken Salad Lunch Wrap

There are many times that we get sick of the same old sandwich every single day. This recipe will certainly give you a break from the normal routine and leave you with a dish that will leave you co-workers jealous.

Calories: 220
Serving Size: 4

Ingredients:

- 4 Tortillas, Low-Carb
- 3 Tbsp. Of Caesar Salad Dressing, Light
- 4 Cups of Fresh Romaine Lettuce
- 1 ½ Cup of Cooked Chicken, Diced Into Long Strips
- 3 Tbsp. of Fresh Parmesan Cheese, Shredded

Directions:

1. In a small mixing bowl, mix all of your ingredients except for your tortillas. Make sure that you coat the salad evenly with enough dressing.

2. On your tortillas spoon about 1 cup of the salad mix into the center. Fold the wrap according to your preferences and repeat for as many wraps as you are making. Serve and enjoy.

The Ultimate Power Salad

This is one of the most delicious and flavor packed salad recipes you will ever come across. It is not only very filling, but it is also very delicious as well.

Calories: 265
Serving Size: 4

Ingredients:
- ¼ Cup of Dry Pepitas, Roasted
- A Large Bag of Baby Spinach
- ½ Cup of Cranberries, Dried
- 2 Tbsp. of Almonds, Sliced
- 1 Small Apple, Cored and Diced Into Small Pieces
- 7 Ounces of Deli Turkey Breast, Sliced Thinly and Cut Into Thin Strips
- 1/3 Cup of Feta Cheese, Reduced Fat and Crumbled Into Small Pieces

Ingredients For Dressing:

- 1 ½ Tbsp. of Olive Oil
- 1/3 Cup of Balsamic Vinegar

Directions:

1. In a salad bowl, mix all of your ingredients together. Serve generous proportions and enjoy immediately.

Red Pepper and Arugula Panini

Switch up your normal lunch menu with this delicious recipe. This recipe is warm and very filling, leaving you feeling satisfied for the rest of the day.

Calories: 190

Serving Size: 4

Ingredients:

- 12 Fresh Basil Leaves, Large in Size
- 3 Tbsp. of Organic Cottage Cheese, Low-Fat
- 2 tsp. of Fresh Lemon Juice
- 16 Arugula Leaves, Large
- 1 1/3 Ounces of Goat Cheese, Soft
- 1 Clove of Garlic, Minced
- 8 Slices of Fresh Rye Bread
- 1 Small Jar of Red Bell Peppers, Drained and Cut Into Small Pieces
- Dash of Black Pepper For Taste

Directions:

1. In a small bowl combine your goat and cottage cheese, lemon juice, minced garlic and black pepper together until thoroughly combined.

2. On your rye bread spread some of the cheese mixture evenly on each slice. Next ray some of your freshly chopped bell pepper on 4 of the slices. Put sandwiches together.

3. Place each sandwich onto your Panini press and grill for the next 5 minutes or until the sandwich is toasted. Once you remove the sandwiches fill them up immediately with your basil and arugula leaves and serve while still warm.

Savory Ginger and Sweet Potato Soup

Since this recipe only calls for you to use four ingredients, it is one of the easiest recipes you will ever make. Plus, it tastes absolutely amazing.

Calories: 85
Serving Size: 6

Ingredients:

- 1 tsp. of Salt, Low Sodium
- 3 Cups of Water, Filtered
- 3 Sweet Potatoes, Large in size, Peeled and Diced Into Small Pieces
- 2 Tbsp. of Ginger, Juiced and Grated

Directions:

1. In a medium sized pot, add in your water, salt, sweet potatoes and ginger. Cook over medium heat until your sweet potatoes are tender.

2. Once the sweet potatoes are tender transfer your "soup" to a blender and process until the soap becomes smooth in consistency. Serve while warm with a small round of bread of your choice and enjoy.

Veggie and Cheese Pitas

This is a perfect vegetarian dish for any who wish to eat something a little more healthy.

Calories: 170
Serving Size: 8

Ingredients:

- 4 Pita Pockets, Whole Wheat
- ¼ Cup of Sunflower Seeds
- 2 Tbsp. of Mayonnaise, Light
- ½ Cup of Hummus
- 4 Leaves of Romaine Lettuce
- 2 ¼ Ounce of Swiss Cheese, Reduced Fat
- 1 Red Onion, Sliced Into Thin Slices
- 1 Cucumber, Sliced Into Thin Slices
- 1 Tomato, Cut Into Equal Sized Slices

Directions:

1. Make a clean slice into one side of your Pita pocket, making sure you do not cut it all the way through. Set these aside.

2. On each pita spread at least ½ of a Tbsp. of Mayo. Then layer 4 slices of Swiss cheese on top of that. Next spread about 2 Tbsp. of hummus onto each slice of cheese and then sprinkle with 1 Tbsp. of sunflower seeds.

3. Place a layer of lettuce, onion, tomatoes and cucumbers on top of the hummus. Stuff as much of the filling as you can in each sandwich and cut in half. Serve and enjoy.

Traditional Tuna Pasta Salad

There is nothing like enjoy a filling tuna pasta salad on a lazy afternoon. This recipe is incredibly easy to make and it tastes delicious.

Calories: 245
Serving Size: 4

Ingredients:
- 2 Whole Carrots, Diced Into Small Pieces
- 2 Cups of Quinoa Pasta, Uncooked
- ¼ Cup of Onion, Diced Into Small Pieces
- 2 Stalks of Celery, Diced Into Small Pieces
- ¼ Cup of Green Olives, Cut Into Small Pieces
- ½ cup of Red Bell Pepper, Cut Into Tiny Pieces
- 3 Tbsp. of Mayonnaise, Light
- Dash of Black Pepper For Taste
- 11 Ounces of Fresh Tuna, In Water
- ¼ Cup of Plain Greek Yogurt, Fat Free

Directions:

1. Cook your pasta in some boiling water and sauce. Once it is al dente drain and rinse under some cool water.

2. In a separate bowl mix all of your ingredients together until they are all thoroughly combined. Add in your pasta and toss until thoroughly mixed. Serve and enjoy.

Traditional Black Bean Mexican Soup

This soup is not only low-carb, but it is incredibly healthy to make. While only taking a couple of minutes to put together, you will have a recipe that tastes as if it came from a restaurant.

Calories: 170

Serving Size: 7

Ingredients:

- Some cooking spray
- ½ of an Onion, Diced Into Small Pieces
- 1 small Container of Chicken Broth, Low-Sodium
- 2 tsp. of Oil, Canola
- Dash of Black Pepper For Taste
- 1 Pound of Chicken Breasts, Boneless, Skinless and Cut Into Small Cubes
- ½ tsp. of Adobo Seasoning, divided in half
- 1 Tbsp. of Chili Powder

- ½ tsp. of Cumin
- 1, 15 Ounce Can of Black Beans, Drained and Rinsed
- 1, 14.5 Ounce can of Tomatoes, Fire Roasted
- ½ cup of Corn, Frozen

Directions:

1. In a large soup pan, spray a generous amount of cooking spray. Add in your oil and onion and sauté for about 3 minutes or until the onions become translucent.

2. Next add in your chicken and season with about ¼ tsp. of Adobo seasoning and some pepper. Cook your chicken until it is slightly brown in color, which is about 6 to 7 minutes on each side.

3. Add in your remaining ingredients and let your soup simmer for 15 minutes. Serve while piping hot and enjoy.

Mini Pepper and Asparagus Quiche

If you have never made quiche before, there is no need to worry. This is a very simple recipe and you can store these quiches in your fridge to enjoy anytime you want.

Calories: 65

Serves: 12

Ingredients:

- Some cooking spray
- 1 Onion, small and diced into small pieces
- 1 Tbsp. of Olive Oil
- 1 Yellow Bell Pepper, Diced into small pieces and seeded
- Dash of Black Pepper For Taste
- 2 Eggs, Medium in size
- 6 Egg Whites
- 6 Original Laughing Cow Cheese Wedges, Light and Cut Into Halves

- 1/3 Cup of Milk, Skim

Directions:

1. Preheat your oven to 375 degrees.

2. Spray a muffin pan with a generous amount of cooking spray and set aside.

3. In a separate sauté pan over medium heat, spray some more cooking spray and add your olive oil. Next add in your onions, asparagus, and bell pepper and sauté them for at least 7 to 9 minutes or until they are fully cooked through. Season with some salt and set aside for later use.

4. In a medium sized bowl blend together your eggs, egg whites and milk with a whish until completely combined.

5. In your muffin cups distribute your sautéed veggie mix evenly. Then add in your egg mixture over the veggies until they are full. Make sure your muffin cups are not overflowing.

6. Take half of your sliced cheese wedges and press it down into the middle of each muffin cup.

7. Lastly bake your quiches for 20 minutes and serve immediately.

Vegetarian Chili

With the beans and vegetables that are used in this dish, this makes for a meal full of fiber and that tastes delicious. There will be plenty enough left to have for leftovers as well.

Calories: 170

Serves: 8

Ingredients:

- 1 Tbsp. of Oil, Canola
- 1 Green Bell Pepper, Chopped Into Small Pieces
- 4 Whole Carrots, Chopped Into Small Pieces
- 2 Cloves of Garlic, Minced
- 1 Small Zucchini, Chopped Into Small Pieces
- 1 Onion, Medium and Sized and Sliced Into Fine Pieces
- 1 Tbsp. of Chili Powder
- 2, 14.5 Ounce Cans of Diced Tomatoes, No Salt and In Juice

- 1, 16 Ounce Can of Red Kidney Beans, Drained and Rinsed Prior To Using
- 1, 16 ounce Can of Black Beans, Drained and Rinsed Prior To Using
- 1, 15 Ounce Can of Tomato Sauce

Directions:

1. Heat up your canola oil in a large soup pot. Next add in your onions and carrots and sauté until the onions are translucent. Add in your green peppers and zucchini to sauté for an additional 2 minutes.

2. Next add in your garlic and sauté for at least 30 seconds to 1 full minute. Season everything with some chili powder and then add in all of your remaining ingredients. Bring soup to a boil.

3. Cover your soup pot and reduce the heat. Simmer your soup for the next 30 to 35 minutes or until all of your vegetables are tender. Serve while piping hot and enjoy.

Broccoli Cream Soup

This is a healthy recipe to make for lunch or whenever you are feeling too lazy to cook. Serve with a small piece of fresh baguette for dipping.

Calories: 110
Serves: 8

Ingredients:

- 6 Cups of Chicken Stock
- 1 Cup of Half and Half, Fat Free
- 1 ½ pounds of Fresh Broccoli, Chopped Into Small Pieces
- 1 Cup of Onion, Diced Into Small Pieces
- 3 Tbsp. of Olive Oil
- ¼ Cup of Flour, Whole Wheat
- 1 tsp. of White Pepper For Taste

Directions:

1. Wash your fresh broccoli as thoroughly as possible before chopping. Set aside.

2. In a small soup pot bring your chicken stock to a nice rolling boil and add in your chopped broccoli. Reduce heat to a simmer. All to cook until the broccoli become tender. Add your chicken stock and broccoli to a blender and puree until it is a smooth consistency.

3. Next add some olive oil into your pot and allow to heat up. Add in your onion and cook until translucent. Sprinkle in your flour slowly and stir constantly to mix. Next add in some chicken stock into your flour mixture and bring to a hot simmer.

4. Next add in your puree broccoli mixture and the half and half and stir the ingredients until thoroughly mixed. Bring to a simmer and season with a touch of pepper. Serve while still piping hot. Enjoy.

Classic Mediterranean Turkey Wrap

You can easily put this dish together for a fast and hearty lunch. Serve while warm or cold and with some fresh fruit.

Calories: 285
Serves: 4

Ingredients:

- 4 Green Olives, Diced Into Tiny Pieces
- 4 Wraps, Whole Wheat and Heated
- ½ of Cucumber, Peeled and Diced Into Small Pieces
- ¼ Cup of Crumbled Feta Cheese, Reduced Fat
- 12 Ounces of Turkey From The Deli, No Salt
- 8 Tbsp. of Hummus
- 2 Roma Tomatoes, Diced Into Small Pieces

Directions:

1. On your wraps spread 2 Tbsp. of Hummus on each. On top of the hummus lay out 3 ounces of your deli style Turkey slices, ¼ of diced cucumber, ¼ cup of your diced roma tomatoes, 1 fully diced olive, and 1 tbsp. of crumbled feta cheese.

2. Fold the wrap to your liking and immediately enjoy.

Lettuce and Shrimp Wraps

This recipe is a creative and delicious way to enjoy shrimp and will surely impress your family and friends.

Calories: 105
Serves: 7

Ingredients:

- Some cooking spray
- 1 Red Bell pepper, Seeded and Diced Into Small Pieces
- 1 tsp. of Sesame Oil
- 1 Clove of Garlic
- 1 Onion, Small In Size and Diced Into Fine Pieces
- ½ of Avocado, Diced Into Small Pieces
- 1 Pound of Shrimp, Deveined and Peeled
- 1 Tbsp. of Soy Sauce, Reduced Sodium
- 1 Tbsp. of Splenda, Brown Sugar Variety

- 1tsp. of Chili Garlic Paste, Thai-Style

- 1 tsp. of Ginger, Grated

- 1 Tbsp. of Fresh Chives, Chopped

- 7 Large Lettuce Leaves

- 1 Tbsp. of Peanut Butter

- 1 Lime, Small in Size, Juiced and Zested

- ¼ Cup of Chicken Broth, Fat Free and Reduced Sodium

Directions:

1. Add some cooking spray and sesame oil to a pan and sauté your onion and bell peppers until the onions are translucent.

2. Next add in your shrimp and sauté those for at least 2 to 3 minutes.

3. In a separate bowl blend together you chili garlic paste, soy sauce, ginger, brown sugar Splenda, chicken broth, peanut butter, lime zest, garlic and lime juice. Cook until the shrimp is fully cooked through and as soon as the sauce begins to thicken up.

4. Add in your chopped up chives and stir until thoroughly mixed.

5. Add mixture to 1 lettuce leaf (equally divided) and top with some chopped avocado. Serve immediately and enjoy.

Hearty Mozzarella and Chickpea Salad

This recipe is perfect to make during the cold winter months. It will leave you feeling full and still wanting more.

Calories: 155
Serves: 4

Ingredients:

- 1 Cup of Fresh Cherry Tomatoes
- 12 Ounces of Fresh Baby Spinach
- 2.5 Ounces of Fresh Mozzarella, Balls and Drained Completely
- Dash of Salt and Pepper For Taste
- 1 Cup of Canned Chickpea, No Salt
- 2 tsp. of Extra Virgin Olive Oil

Directions:

1. Combine your tomatoes, fresh mozzarella balls and chickpeas in a small to medium sized bowl. Add a touch of olive oil and stir completely to combine. Sprinkle with some salt and pepper for taste.

2. Wash your baby spinach and layer it delicately onto a bowl. Place your tomato, chickpea and mozzarella mixture on top of your baby spinach. Serve and enjoy.

Spicy Watermelon Salad With Baked Catfish

This recipe is great to serve alongside a small salad or a cup of fruit and is welcoming to have for lunch or dinner.

Calories: 360
Serves: 4

Ingredients:
- 1 Whole Lime
- Dash of Salt and Pepper For Taste
- 1 tsp. of Olive Oil
- 4 Fillets of Catfish
- 1 Tbsp. of Honey
- ¼ of Red Onion, Sliced Into Thin Slices
- 1 Jalapeno Pepper, Chopped Into Small Pieces
- ¼ Cup of Fresh Cilantro, Chopped Into Fine Pieces
- 2 ½ Pounds of Seedless Watermelon, Chopped Into Small Cubes

- ½ tsp. of Cumin, Ground

Directions:

1. Preheat your over to 350 degrees.

2. In a Large bowl zest some of your lime into it. Next Cut your lime in half and squeeze as much juice as you can from one of the halves into the bowl.

3. Next add in your olive oil, cumin, pepper and salt into your lime mixture and stir thoroughly to combine. Transfer mixture into a baking dish and mix again.

4. Next place your fillets of catfish into the baking dish and turn over onto both sides to coat evenly with your lime mixture. Place into your oven and bake for 15 minutes or until your catfish turns opaque in color or if it flakes off when you scrape it with a fork.

5. Lastly take the remaining half of your lime and squeeze the juice out into another bowl. Add your honey and whisk together. Next add in your watermelon cubes, cilantro, onion, pepper and toss to coat evenly. Serve with your catfish fillets and enjoy.

Chicken in Tomato Basil Soup

If you want to double up the ingredients on this recipe to make enough for leftovers, feel free to do so.

Calories: 195
Serves: 4

Ingredients:

- ¼ Cup of Mozzarella Cheese, Shredded
- 1, 14.5 Ounce Can of Diced Tomatoes, Seasoned With Italian Seasoning
- 1 tsp. of Sugar
- 2 Package of Chicken Breasts, Boneless and Skinless
- 1/2, 15.5 Ounce Can of Navy Beans, No Salt, Drained and Rinsed
- 2 tsp. of Extra Virgin Olive Oil
- 2 Ounces of Baby Spinach Leaves
- 1 Can of Chicken Broth, Reduced Sodium

- 2 Tbsp. of Fresh Basil Leaves, Chopped Into Fine Pieces

Directions:

1. Combine your beans, sugar, tomatoes and chicken broth in a saucepan. Bring to a rolling boil for 5 minutes and reduce heat.

2. Next add in your chicken, basil and baby spinach. Cook until your baby spinach becomes wilted and remove from heat. Drizzle in your oil.

3. Serve and top with a generous amount of shredded Mozzarella Cheese and enjoy.

Black Bean Vegetarian Burgers

With this recipe you will never want to buy frozen veggie burgers again. These burgers are delicious, very filling and will leave you wanting more.

Calories: 200
Serves: 4

Ingredients:

- 1, 16 Ounce Can of Black Beans, Rinsed and Drained
- 3 Cloves of Garlic, Peeled and Cut Into Fine Pieces
- 1 Egg
- 1 Tbsp. of Cumin
- 1 Tbsp. of Chili Powder
- ½ Of Green Bell pepper, Cut into Tiny Pieces
- 1 tsp. of Your Favorite Hot Sauce
- ½ of Onion, Cut Into Thin Wedges
- ½ Cup of Bread Crumbs

Directions

1. Preheat your grill and cover one rack with a sheet of aluminum foil.

2. In a medium sized bowl, mash your black beans with a fork until they become pasty in consistency.

3. In a blender or food processor, chop up your bell pepper, garlic and onions until it is finely chopped.

4. In a separate bowl mix your egg, chili powder, chili sauce and cumin together until thoroughly combined. Add into your mashed bean mixture and mix in your bread crumbs. Your mixture should now hold together. Divide this mixture into four generous sized patties.

5. Place patties onto your grill for about 8 minutes on each side or to your liking. Then place on hamburger buns and thoroughly enjoy.

Nutritious Spinach and Pasta Shells

This recipe is perfect for those who do not eat pasta too much, but enjoy a touch of garlic and spices with their pasta. This dish goes great with a salad or a small bowl of fruit.

Calories: 310
Serves: 8

Ingredients:

- Dash of Salt For Taste
- 1 Pound of Seashell Shaped Pasta
- 2 Tbsp. of Extra Virgin Olive Oil
- 1 tsp. of Red Pepper Flakes, Dried
- 1 Package frozen Spinach, Chopped
- 7 tsp. of Garlic, Minced

Directions:

1. Bring a large pot of water with some salt added in to a nice rolling boil. Add in your pasta and frozen spinach. Cook until pasta is al dente and drain.

2. In a separate skillet heat up your olive oil. Add in your garlic and red pepper flakes to sauté for the next 5 minutes or until the minced garlic begins to turn gold in color. Add your cooked pasta and spinach to the pan and mix thoroughly. Remove from heat and serve with a touch of salt. Enjoy.

Delicious Desserts

Yummy Quinoa Pudding

This quinoa pudding is a real treat to have during the holidays and is one of those desserts that is high in protein.

Calories: 250

Serves: 6

Ingredients:

- 1 Cup of Quinoa (Rinse before using)
- 1 ½ Cup of Milk, Skim
- 1 tsp. of Vanilla
- ½ Cup of Pumpkin Seeds
- ½ tsp. of Cinnamon, Ground
- 1 ½ cup Half and Half, Fat-Free
- ¼ tsp. of Nutmeg, Ground
- ¼ Cup of Brown Sugar Splenda

Directions:

1. Wash your quinoa under cold running water for as long as 2 minutes.

2. In a medium sized saucepan whisk together your half and hald, vanilla, milk, brown sugar Splenda, nutmeg and cinnamon until thoroughly combined. Bring to a simmer over medium heat.

3. The moment your mixture comes to a simmer, add in your quinoa and reduce the heat to low. Cover your pan halfway and cook for the next 40 minutes, making sure to stir as often as every 10 minutes.

4. After 40 minutes stir in your pumpkin seeds and serve while still piping hot.

Watermelon and Strawberry Frozen Dessert

For a light and nutritious dessert, this is certainly the recipe for you.

Calories: 50
Serves: 8

Ingredients:

- ¼ Cup of Water
- 1/3 Cup of Domino Light
- 1 Tbsp. of Lime Juice, Freshly Squeezed
- 4 Cups of Fresh Watermelon, Seeded and Cut Into Small Chunks
- 1 1/3 Cup of Fresh Strawberry, Washed and Hulled

Directions:

1. In a separate saucepan over medium to high heat, combine your water and Domino Light together with a whisk. Keep whisking until mixture begins to boil. As soon as it comes to a boil reduce heat to a simmer and cook for another 4 minutes. Remove from heat.

2. In a blender combine your strawberries and watermelon together. Puree together until it becomes a creamy consistency. Next add in your lime juice. Add as much Domino Light and Lime Juice as you want until you are satisfied with the sweetness.

3. Pour your entire mixture in a large bowl and cover with some plastic wrap. Store in your fridge for the next 2 hours to chill. Transfer to your freezer and let sit for 1 hour.

4. Serve in ice cream bowl and enjoy.

Pumpkin Panna Cotta

If you do not know what Panna Cotta is, it is a custard like dessert that is absolutely delicious. This recipe is perfect to make during the holidays and will surely impress your friends and family.

Calories: 75
Serves: 8

Ingredients:

- 1 Cup of Milk, Skim
- ½ Cup of Whipped Topping, Fat Free
- ½ Cup of Buttermilk, Low Fat
- 8, 4 Ounce Dessert Cups
- ¼ Cup of Brown Sugar Splenda
- 1, 15 Ounce Can of Pumpkin, Puree
- 1 Packet of Gelatin, Unflavored
- ½ Cup of Plain Greek Yogurt, Non-Fat
- 2 tsp. of Pumpkin Pie Spice

Directions:

1. Whisk together your buttermilk, milk, unflavored gelatin and Splenda brown sugar in a saucepan. Let it sit unheated for 5 minutes.

2. In a separate medium sized bowl, whisk together your pumpkin pie spice, puree pumpkin and Greek yogurt together. Set this aside for later use.

3. Add in some hot milk mixture into your pumpkin mixture next and whisk thoroughly until consistency is smooth. Next divide up your mixture into your dessert cups and refrigerate for at least 1 hour or overnight for best results.

4. When serving top each dessert cup with 1 Tbsp. of Whipped topping.

Berry and Chocolate Parfait

This is the perfect recipe to make for Valentine's day and will leave your Valentine feeling special.

Calories: 115
Serves: 6

Ingredients:

- ¾ Cup of Fresh Blueberries
- 1.4 Ounce of Pudding, Sugar Free and Fat Free
- 2 Cups of Milk, Nonfat
- ¾ Cup of Strawberries, Sliced Into Thin Pieces
- 4 Ounces and 12 Tbsp. of Whipped Topping, Fat Free

Directions:

1. In a medium sized bowl, blend together your pudding and milk with a whisk and then fold in 4 ounces of your whipped topping

2. In a small parfait dish layer your dessert with ¼ cup of the pudding mixture, then layer on 2 Tbsp. of strawberries, then 2 Tbsp. of blueberries and then another layer of ¼ cup of your pudding mixture.

3. Continue this process for the rest of the servings you have and serve while chilled.

Smore Shooters

This is another great recipe to make for your significant other for Valentine's day.

Calories: 140

Serves: 4

Ingredients:

- 4 tsp. of Mini Chocolate Chips
- 2 Cups of Milk, Skim
- 4 Small Dessert Glasses
- 1, 1.4 Ounce of Instant Chocolate Pudding Mix
- 1 ½ Graham Cracker Sheets
- 8 Tbsp. of Whipped Topping, Light

Directions:

1. In a medium sized bowl combine together your pudding and skim milk using a whisk. Place in your refrigerator for 5 minutes to chill.

2. Next place your graham cracker sheets into a plastic bag and crush until they are tiny crumbs.

3. Next place ¼ cup of your pudding mix into the bottom of your dessert glass. Next top it with 1 Tbsp. of Your graham cracker and finish with a topping of whipped Cream. Sprinkle with a few mini chocolate chips and serve while still cold.

Delicious Mini Pumpkin Tarts

When you first look at this recipe, you will never believe that it is a diabetic recipe. These tarts are simply delicious and will surely impress your guests.

Calories: 40
Serves: 30

Ingredients:

- 30 Mini Wafer Cookies of Your Choice
- 1 Egg
- 8 Ounces of Softened Cream Cheese, Light
- ½ tsp. of Cinnamon
- Pinch of Nutmeg
- ¼ Cup of Sour Cream, Light
- ½ tsp. of Vanilla
- ¾ Cup of Canned Pumpkin
- ¼ Cup of Splenda

Directions:

1. Preheat your oven to 350 degrees. While it heats up line a muffin tin pan with baking cups.

2. In a separate medium sized bowl add all of your ingredients together and mix with an electric mixture until the batter is smooth.

3. Fill each muffin cup ¾ of the way and bake for the next 30 minutes. Once it has finished baking let it cool completely before serving.

Traditional Apple Crisp

If you are looking for a traditional apple crisp recipe that will be healthy and al around safe to eat, this is the recipe for you.

Calories: 145
Serves: 7

Ingredients:
- Some cooking spray
- 5 Cups of Apples, Peeled and Sliced
- ¼ Cup of Brown Sugar, Packed
- 1 tsp. of Vanilla
- ¼ Cup of Flour, All-Purpose
- ½ tsp. of Nutmeg, Ground
- ½ Cup of Oats, Old-Fashioned
- 1 tsp. of Cinnamon, Ground
- 2 Tbsp. of Margarine, Softened Prior To Use

Directions:

1. Preheat your oven to 375 degrees and coat a baking pan with some cooking spray.

2. In a small mixing bowl, mix your brown sugar, oats, nutmeg, flour, cinnamon and vanilla together until thoroughly combined.

3. Layer your sliced apples in your baking pan and coat with your brown sugar mixture until thoroughly coated. Back for 30 minutes and serve while warm.

Delicious Trifle Pudding

This dessert is a crowd pleasing favorite especially during the 4th of July. It is incredibly easy to make and takes absolutely delicious.

Calories: 75
Serves: 16

Ingredients:

- 1 ½ Cup of Strawberries, Sliced
- 2 Cups of Milk, Fat Free
- 1 Ounce of Vanilla Pudding, Sugar Free and Fat Free
- 2 ½ Cups of Fresh Blueberries
- 2 ½ Cup of Fresh Raspberries
- 8 Ounce of Whipped Topping, Light

Directions:

1. In a large mixing bowl empty out your vanilla pudding and cool in your refrigerator for a couple of minutes.

2. Next fold in your whipped topping into the pudding and mix until thoroughly combined.

3. In a trifle bowl put your pudding, then raspberries, then pudding, then blueberries, then pudding then strawberries. Continue with this layering until trifle bowl is full and top with some whipped topping.

Low Fat Style Crème Brule

You do not need to be the next Iron Chef in order to make Crème Brule. With this recipe you can make crème Brule that is delicious and completely healthy.

Calories: 115
Serves: 4

Ingredients:
- 2 Egg Whites,
- 1 Egg
- 12 Fresh Raspberries
- 1 Cup of Milk, Skim
- 2 Cups of Water, Hot
- 1 tsp. of Vanilla
- ¼ Cup of Greek Yogurt, Non Fat
- ¼ Cup plus 2 tsp. of Splenda

Directions:

1. Preheat your oven to 350 degrees.

2. In a medium sized bowl combine your milk, egg whites, vanilla, egg, Splenda and yogurt together with a whisk.

3. Using a casserole dish place your dessert dishes into them and fill the baking dish with some water, without pouring it into the dessert dish. Pour your dessert batter into your dessert dishes and place into your oven.

4. Bake for the next 40 minutes. Once finished remove your dessert dishes from your pan and place them to refrigerate in your fridge for at least 24 hours.

5. Serve while still cool and enjoy.

Mouthwatering Frozen Greek Yogurt

You can serve this yogurt with your favorite type of fruit to make this dessert dish more personal for you.

Calories: 70
Serves: 6

Ingredients:

- ½ Cup of Splenda
- 3 Cups of Plain Greek Yogurt, Non-Fat
- 1 Sprig of Thyme, Fresh
- 1 Lemon, Juiced and Zested
- 2 Tbsp. of Water

Directions:

1. Combine all of your ingredients except for the Greek yogurt and mix until thoroughly combined. Place into a small pan and heat up to a boil. Remove from heat and remove your sprig of thyme.

2. Once your lemon mixture is cooled whisk this together with your greek yogurt. Churn together until the mixture becomes thick an then place into your freezer. Once frozen serve immediately. Enjoy.

Almond Flavored Hot Chocolate

If you are a fan of almonds and hot chocolate, this recipe is certainly going to appeal to you.

Calories: 105
Serves: 4

Ingredients:

- 1/4 Cup of Almonds, Sliced
- ½ Cup of Whipped Topping, Fat Free
- ¼ Cup of Cocoa Powder
- ½ tsp. Coconut Extract
- 4 Cups of Almond Milk, Unsweetened
- ¼ Cup Of Splenda Sugar

Directions:

1. In a saucepan add your almonds over medium heat and toasted lightly. Set these aside to cool off.

2. Next add in your almond milk, cocoa powder, splenda and coconut and blended together until the entire mixture becomes foamy.

3. Next add your hot chocolate mixture to your saucepan and heat up over medium heat. Serve into a small coffee mug and sprinkle with toasted almonds. Enjoy.

Baked Cinnamon Apples

Once you begin baking these delicious apples, it will leave you mouth watering until you give these a taste.

Calories: 145
Serves: 4

Ingredients:

- ¼ Cup of Pecans, Chopped Finely
- 1 tsp. of Cinnamon
- 2 Tbsp. of Margarine, Trans Fat Free
- 4 Large Apples of Your Choice, Peeled and Cored
- ¼ Cup Oatmeal
- ½ of a Lemon, Juiced
- ¼ Cup and 2 Tbsp. of Splenda Brown Sugar

Directions:

1. Preheat your oven to 425 degrees. Place your apples in a oven safe dish and drizzle them with some lemon juice.

2. In a small mixing bowl mix all of your remaining ingredients and once thoroughly combined, stuff each apple with your mixture.

3. Bake your apples for 25 to 30 degrees and allow to cool before serving. Enjoy.

Pumpkin Bread Pudding

This is another traditional holiday dessert that you can make to impress your friends and family.

Calories: 140

Serves: 4

Ingredients:

- 1 Egg
- 1 Egg White
- 2 Tsp. of Pecans, Chopped
- 3 Cups of French Bread, Cut Into Small Cubes
- 2/3 Cup of Milk, 1% Low Fat
- 1 tsp. of Vanilla
- ¼ tsp. of Cinnamon, Ground
- ¼ tsp. of Pumpkin Pie Spice
- ¼ Cup of Pumpkin, Canned
- 8 Packets of Splenda

Directions:

1. Preheat your oven to 350 degrees. Spray 4 oven safe dessert dishes with some cooking spray and set aside until you are ready to use it.

2. Mix your milk, pumpkin, egg, egg whites, splenda, various spices and vanilla together with a whisk and then add in your chopped up pieces of bread. Stir and let bread to soak for at least 10 to 15 minutes.

3. Place this mixture into the your greased dessert dishes and top with your chopped pecans. Bake your pudding for 10 minutes and place aluminum foil on it for it to back for another 10-15 minutes. You can served immediately or wait until they are chilled.

Strawberries Dipped In Balsamic Vinegar

This recipe will give you a creative and unique way to making a delicious summer dessert.

Calories: 110
Serves: 6

Ingredients:

- 2 Tbsp. of Balsamic Vinegar
- ¼ tsp. of Black Pepper, For Taste
- 16 Ounces of Fresh Strawberries, Hulled and Cut In Half
- ¼ Cup of Sugar

Directions:

1. Place your strawberries into a bowl and drizzle the vinegar over them.

2. Sprinkle with some sugar and stir very gently to combine thoroughly.

3. Cover with some plastic wrap and let it sit at room temperature for at least an hour. Serve and enjoy with a sprinkle of black pepper.

Banana and Chocolate Tofu Pudding

This delicious tasting dessert is easy enough to whip up in about 5 minutes flat and it will please any sweet tooth.

Calories: 230
Serves: 4

Ingredients:

- 1 Banana, Peeled and broken Into Small Chunks
- ¼ Cup of Powdered Sugar
- 3 Tbsp. of Milk, Soy
- 1 Package of Tofu, Soft and Silken
- 5 Tbsp. of Cocoa Powdered, Unsweetened
- Pinch of Cinnamon, Ground

Directions:

1. In a blender combine all of your ingredients and blend until smooth or to your preference.

2. Refrigerate for 1 hour and then serve while chilled.

Sugar Free Applesauce Cake

This is a great tasting recipe for diabetics and for those who just wish to enjoy a dessert dish that is healthy.

Calories: 240
Serves: 4

Ingredients:
- ½ tsp. of Slat
- 2 Cups of Flour, All-Purpose
- ½ tsp. of Cinnamon
- 1 tsp. of Baking Powder
- ½ tsp. of Nutmeg, ground
- 1 tsp. of Baking Soda
- ½ Cup of Fresh Raisins
- 2 Eggs
- 1 ½ Cup of Applesauce, Unsweetened
- 1 tsp. of Vanilla
- ¾ Cup of Brown Sugar

Directions:

1. Preheat your oven to 350 degrees and spray a cake pan with a generous amount of cooking spray. Set aside.

2. Next Combine your flour, baking soda, salt, cinnamon, nutmeg and baking powder together until fully mixed. Set to the side.

3. Next beat your eggs until they are light and fluffy and add in your brown sugar. Then add in your unsweetened applesauce and vanilla. Mix thoroughly to combine. Fold in raisins and powdered ingredients and mix into a thick batter.

4. Pour your batter into your greased cake pan and bake at 350 degrees for one hour or until the cake sets. Test with toothpick or butter knife. Enjoy.

Hey one more thing!

I hope you enjoyed the recipes, and please feel free to leave a review if you did! That would be greatly appreciated!

I have been creating recipes of all kinds over the years for my mother and am only trying to share them with others who may suffer from diabetes.

I am not claiming to be a Doctor or even an expert chef, I am only trying to help out others who may be looking for variety and healthy choices in their diets.

Thanks for reading!
Maria

Printed in Great Britain
by Amazon